Writing Your Bible

MICHAEL W. TEMPLE

ISBN 979-8-89043-162-2 (paperback)
ISBN 979-8-89043-163-9 (digital)

Christian Faith Publishing
832 Park Avenue
Meadville, PA 16335
www.christianfaithpublishing.com

Printed in the United States of America

PROLOGUE

Prior to my divorce in 2004, I called up a friend named Jeff, who lived in Missouri. We talked about old times. And during the course of the conversation, I opened my heart to Jeff. I said, "Jeff, I want to serve God. The problem is, I know I have a lot to work on myself. I have a lot flaws. There are things that I must get fixed in my life before I can serve Him.

"So, what you are telling me…is…you…have to get perfect…before *God*…can use you in His kingdom. Is that what I am hearing you say?"

Jeff always had the perfect pauses to put things into perspective. He was a masterful salesperson who knew every technique for making a person think about what they were really saying and if it was in fact logical or coherent. That is much of selling a product, the idea of getting someone to think about the logical extreme.

I was caught like a deer in the headlights. "Uh…uh…uh, yes, I guess that is what I am saying." I surrendered in embarrassment as I thought it through. I would not and could not ever be perfect, but that was my rationale. It was absurd.

"Well, that is the most idiotic thing I have ever heard come across your lips buddy!" he said rather smugly. Jeff was not afraid to call a spade a dirty old shovel.

I bring this conversation up to inoculate you, the reader, to the once-ridiculous thought process that I had, which may cripple you the same had I not brought this to your attention aforehand. Please do not think for an instance that using the argument that you must wait for perfection to service God is a legitimate defense for procrastination. This is simply hogwash. In fact, as you search the Bible from Abraham to Paul, you will never find a perfect servant free from sin. You are no different, and so I implore you to press on regardless of your sin or shortcomings. Had I waited to be perfect, I would have never written two books or fathered eleven additional children.

We are all a work in progress and thankful for the grace that saves us. Take your steps to help others in humility, knowing God has let you proceed despite your flaws yet in confidence, knowing His kingdom is better for your efforts. You may have more or less mistakes in your past or present than myself. This isn't a game of casting guilt. Satan is the accuser of the brethren. Let us be an encourager of the brethren in all circumstances. In plain terms, we all suck without the special cloak of Yeshua wrapped around us. As others see good or great in us, then let it be deferred to the image of Yeshua. When we are weak, let us depend carefully on the arms of Him who knows our weakness and strength.

I hope, as you read these words, you will not become frightened to read on but rather encouraged to seek the guidance of my loving instruction in the pages that follow.

Bless you for taking time to read this book!

CHAPTER 1

Groceries

"WHEN YOU PRAY to God, you must be precise in your prayer!" the pastor boldly professed from the pulpit. "Tell God exactly what your need is. If you need a truck with a hitch, then tell him. If it needs to have a V8 engine, then tell him. If you need $345 to meet your electric bill that is past due, then tell him."

Brother Mac was a Southern Baptist pastor who prayed in King James English and sweated profusely while preaching in this tiny un-air-conditioned brick church.

I lay on the pew, chewing Doublemint gum, watching my mother wave a church bulletin quickly while beads of sweat rolled off her nose. She patted my leg like a mom does to console an anxious youngster who doesn't have the patience to get through a Sunday night sermon in ninety-degree heat.

Mom and I arrived home around 8:00 p.m., and Mom said to me, "Michael, we are going to do exactly what Brother Mac said to do. Come over here and help me with this list."

Because of circumstances out of my mother's control, we were without food. Literally, the cupboards were bare, and the fridge was empty. We were in a bad place. Mom began to write a grocery list in her perfect cursive penmanship. She and I composed a list of probably eighty to one hundred items we needed. It's easy to think of a lot of food items when you're hungry. I chimed in things every youngster wants but usually doesn't get, especially when you are in poverty. After we completed the list, Mom said, "Now we are going to pray. Lord, you know our needs, and we have listed out specifically what groceries we need today. Please provide for our needs. Amen."

Knock knock, someone was at the door. Mom opened the door, and my first sight was brown paper bags. They were in the arms of a lady named Zila Seul, who went to our church. She brought in many other bags, and of course, Mom had tears in her eyes while she laughed heartily, telling Zila how we had just finished praying for groceries when she knocked at the door. Nearly every item on our list was contained in these grocery bags, quite to our amazement. It was such a great feeling. You could see God's fingerprints all over this event.

As a first grader, this was probably the first miracle I witnessed in my life, and of course, it had a big impact on me for the rest of my life. I have recounted this story to dozens of people through the years in my witness of God's power and provision.

Many people have heard the stories of Jesus, whom I call Yeshua, feeding thousands with a few fish and some loaves of bread. This is a wonderful story, and yet this was a couple of thousand years ago. The story is true. But what I have found is that the story of my grocery miracle seems to resonate and move people more than the story in the Bible. They are both true stories, but somehow, firsthand knowledge of God's intervention seems to be more poignant to the people that hear the story. This effect made me reflect on how the events in the Bible happened to ordinary people, just like you and me. Then the thought occurred to me that we should all be recording these acts of God for ourselves in order to share with others. In simple terms, we should all be writing our own Bible for others to read.

So as I share some more of my own miracles and stories of God's intervention in my life throughout the following pages, I will separate these into specific categories and also speak to the effects of writing your Bible on others in your life. My prayer is that you will literally put this advice into practice and affect change in millions of people's lives for the good of the kingdom and the salvation of others.

CHAPTER 2

The Water Bill

I HAD BEEN selling smoke alarms for almost a year but with very little success. I had spent over $30,000 in savings to keep food on the table, utilities on, and the mortgage paid. The day came when all the money was gone, and the disconnection notice showed up for the water bill. I prayed about the bill, and I distinctly heard God say to me in my mind, "I've got it covered."

The notice had arrived on a Monday or Tuesday, giving us a few days to pay it or get the water turned off. Friday came, and the water didn't shut off. Whew, at least we had the weekend with water and maybe something would happen over the weekend where we would get some money. I had been applying for jobs left and right, but most places kept saying, "You're overqualified," which is the last thing you want to hear when all you want is to put some food on the table, and you don't care about titles.

Monday came, and the water was still on. Tuesday morning came, and I woke up with a desire to do something I had thought of doing for months but procrastinated on. I had this idea to create my own Bible tracts that were written by me with my message. I wrote out a tract that fit on a small note card, and I printed about twelve of them out to take with me that day. The message on the tract read something like, "Challenge God to a miracle, and He will respond because He loves you and wants you to know He is real." I came upstairs from my office and sat down on the couch, proud of my new Bible tract.

Michelle turned on the water in the kitchen, and all you could hear was hissing and stuttered vibrations in the absence of water. Michelle came into the living room and sat down on the sofa across from me.

"Mike, what are we going to do?" she pleaded.

I looked at her, and all I could think was that I heard God say He had it covered. "Michelle, I swear to you, I heard God say to me He had it covered."

"Mike, we have a lot of kids. We can't go without water," she pressed me.

So at this point, I did what many people do in a jam. I went to my garage and prayed, looking up in the darkness. I said very emphatically, "God you have to help me out here. My faith is weak. I thought You told me you had it covered. You have got to give me something to keep my faith together!"

Instantly, like a lightning bolt, a Bible chapter and verse flashed in my mind. It wasn't the words but just Psalm 29:10. I left the garage and opened the sliding glass door to the kitchen. Nervously, I shouted to Michelle, "Hey, look up this verse for me. It's Psalm 29, verse 10." I closed the door and went back up to the backyard where I would pace and try to think of ways to make some quick cash. After a little bit, I returned to the kitchen and asked her what the verse said. She stated with a little smile, "It says that, basically, He is Lord over the floodwaters."

It is difficult to put peace like this into words. But when she said that to me, peace took over my cells. My body went to complete rest. Anxiety fled away. I knew that I knew that I knew my Daddy was in control. I was so grateful for what God did before He did what He did. We can truly count on Him. He knows the end from the beginning and all points in between.

I went back outside to just ponder the miracle of what just happened. In less than thirty minutes, Michelle opened the sliding glass door with the biggest smile on her face, holding a check and a ziplock bag full of change in her hand. "This check just showed up in the mail. Here is all the change I could find in the couches and around the house. Now go pay the water bill!"

It was a check for something like $181.55 from a customer. We had financed the purchase of some smoke alarms for this customer because the finance company had declined their financing due to credit issues. They had not been paying, and I thought we would just have to write off the loan as a bad debt.

As I was driving to the credit union, I heard God's voice say, "Just take out $175." So when I got to the credit union, I cashed in the coins at the kiosk and took the receipt to the clerk. I deposited the check, withdrew $175, and got the money for the change, which was something like $8 and some change. I went across the street and tried to put in $1 worth of gas. I failed and accidentally put in $2. I know this is funny to some people, but when you are broke, every little decision seems so important.

I had never had my water shut off before. Silly me, I thought that you walked in to pay the bill, discreetly shuffling out the door without a soul knowing you were so poor your water was shut off. Nope, that's not how it works, at least not in my town.

"I need to pay my bill," I stated to the clerk.

She pulled up my info and said, "You will need to talk with one of our staff to get this back on. Please have a seat over there."

A lady came out to get me and showed me back to her desk. I didn't have a water bill with me, so I stated very humbly, "Ma'am, I don't even know how much we owe."

She looked at the computer screen intently and said slowly, "It shows you owe $181.25."

Immediately and without thinking, I responded, "Oh, He was off a little bit."

She responded in with a snotty tone, "I don't show in the notes where you talked to anyone here at our office to get an amount."

My mind was just a fabulous whirlwind, contemplating that God had a check come in the mail that was within pennies of the correct amount, then told me to take out only $175, knowing the exact amount of change in the bag, the gasoline error, and the exact amount of my bill, which I did not know even. *How incredible*! I stated in defense, "Oh no, I meant God!"

Her eyes rolled back in her head. I could see her thoughts that this was one of the nutjobs that hears God. I wasn't about to back down now.

"No, really, look at this." I showed her the receipt where I just deposited the check thirty minutes earlier and explained that we didn't have any money until that check showed up an hour ago. She seemed unchanged by my testimony. I left one of my tracts on her desk upside down. Maybe I reached her. I probably will never know.

CHAPTER 3

Thunder Van

WHEN MICHELLE AND I got married, we had eight children starting off. She had twin boys that were three and a little nine-month-old girl. I had five daughters and no boys.

I told God, as I was driving to work the first morning after we were married, that I was going to need a vehicle more suitable for our family. When I arrived at work that day, one of the ladies in my department said, "Mike, what you really need is a church van, one of those vans that is extra long."

I told her she was right.

Later that day, I received a call from a man named Ernie, who went to my church and was a character in the Passion play that I had a part in as a beggar with crippled legs. Ernie had called in, asking for a payoff amount on his furniture loan. I pulled up the amount and told him what was still owed. He thanked me for the help. And as I was ready to hang up, Ernie asked me, "Mike, you don't happen to need a vehicle, do you?"

Stunned by his question, I replied, "Well, in fact I do, Ernie. I just got married, and I need a big van, something like a church van, like they pick up people with to go to church."

"Well, I think I might have something that matches your need exactly. I'll call you back in a minute," he stated.

About five minutes later, Ernie was on the phone again. "Mike, we have this big, white Dodge van that interestingly was traded in by Celebration's First Assembly of God in Waterloo. I can bring it up for you to see if you like," he offered. Absolutely, bring it on.

Ernie pulled into the furniture store parking lot and asked me if I wanted to drive it to see if it was right. I had been thinking about the fact that I had prayed that morning, and within hours, a man I knew from church, out of the blue, asked me if I needed a vehicle. What are the odds of that?

I told Ernie, "No, Ernie, I don't need to drive this vehicle. God brought this to me, and I trust Him. Just write up the paperwork, and we will be down to Iowa City later today to pick it up."

The van was exactly what we needed. It was a fifteen-passenger with nice red seats and rubberized floor that was easy to clean. It was old, but it ran great, and we had great service from that van for many years. We affectionately called her "the Thunder Van" because even though it was in great condition, the roof had a support that had failed. And when you hit railroad tracks, it would flex and make a sound like thunder. The kids really got a kick out of that.

Once again, I could see God's fingerprints on this wonderful miracle of provision, and my faith increased that day.

CHAPTER 4

Ride from Camp

EVERY YEAR, OUR family celebrates the Feast of Tabernacles, or sometimes it's called the Feast of Succoth. Yeshua fulfilled this feast by coming to dwell with us, and we commemorate this fact by camping out for eight days each fall.

One year we camped out at a campground outside Altoona, Iowa. It was a great week, and the kids had a blast building fires, fishing, roasting marshmallows, and singing songs at our nightly group worship services.

This was a year that was financially lean for us, and we were down to no money. It was time to head home, and I knew we didn't have any money to buy gas. The needle on the fuel tank was barely over empty. Of course, the big Thunder Van, with its big V8 engine, would drink gas so fast you could virtually watch the needle drop while you drove.

We loaded up to leave for home. I kept thinking to myself, *I know God is a last-minute God. He comes through at just in time to save the day.* I think He does this sometimes to build our faith in Him. It is certainly tough to have faith when it seems nothing seems to be working out, and you're in the final hour, so to speak. We got as far as the entry ramp to Interstate 80 East, and my cell phone rang.

Aha! I knew it. He is coming through with the gas money just when we have to get on the highway. This must be the answer. It was a call from a business partner in Des Moines, and I thought, surely he must be calling me to say he had money for me or something like that. Nope. I was wrong.

I looked at Michelle, and she said, "So what are we going to do? We know this isn't enough fuel to get us back an-hour-and-a-half drive to Cedar Rapids."

"I don't know. I am just going to drive," I replied, sounding like a fool. I just didn't know what to do. I didn't have a good answer or some brilliant plan. What I knew in my heart was that God had never let me down, and I really didn't think He was going to start that day. Michelle and I had been in some pretty tough situations, and we never went begging. God just came through, and admittedly, He used other people to help us, but it wasn't because of our own doing. It was because of His merciful, loving nature that sees our needs ahead of our own experience. He knew we were going to be almost out of gas years ago.

I started driving down the road, and of course, it was hard to not look at the needle. We drove for a while, and I role-played in my mind how maybe we would run out of gas along the highway, and some Good Samaritan sent by God would stop to help us. I had a van full of precious cargo, and I really needed Him to come through, but I wasn't sure how this was going to play out. I just kept driving.

After maybe forty to forty-five minutes, I started to look to my left at the beautiful white, puffy clouds against the backdrop of gorgeous blue skies. I have always loved looking at clouds. When I paint pictures, I love to paint clouds. As I kept driving, occasionally I would look to my left again and take in the scenery and splendor of such a beautiful autumn day. After doing this a few times, something occurred to me that was so subtle that it could have been easily missed by anyone just running through life with no God sensors on. In this instance, I realized there was a particular cloud that had managed to keep pace with our van traveling at seventy miles per hour. It was moving along a parallel course, with Interstate 80 right beside us! I drove another five miles and checked again, and it was still there. By this point, I had to say something to Michelle.

"Michelle, I might be crazy. Look over at that cloud. Do you see that? That cloud has been even with our van for a long time. I don't get how that could happen," I explained to her. We kept driving, and the cloud just stayed right beside us the whole way to Iowa City. And, yes, we had no gas. And, yes, our engine kept going. I just kept driving, enthralled by how this cloud could keep up with us.

We reached the I-380 interchange, where we would take a clover leaf and head north to Cedar Rapids. To my wonderment, the cloud stayed with us as we headed north. By this point, everyone in the van was in astonishment, and we were on a Holy Spirit high, just marveling that we just drove from Altoona to Cedar Rapids with a tank on empty. As I pulled into the house on Ozark, I leaped from the van and began to dance around the front yard in a celebration that we made it by the hand of a mighty God. I'm sure the neighbors thought I was a weirdo that day, which is fine with me.

He makes a way when there seems to be no way. Sometimes we have to forget whether something is rational or logical in order to set the stage for God to do His handiwork. He works outside our physical parameters, and this is hard to really comprehend.

CHAPTER 5

The Good Times Motel

MY CHILDHOOD WAS filled with many things that a young person should not have to go through. My father and mother were married for eleven years and were separated eleven times in that period of time. My father had problems with nearly every vice a person can imagine, and one of them was infidelity.

My mother would drive us to church every Wednesday night, Sunday morning, and Sunday evening. Saturday mornings we drove to do laundry at the laundromat in Waterloo. We lived on a farm, and we would drive through the little town of Washburn and then through Waterloo to our destination.

I was too young to know what a brothel was at the time. I can only remember my mother saying that this particular motel that was on our route was a bad place. Years later, I found out that my mother hated this place because of the sins committed there, but more importantly that my father was a client.

Even though things get foggy over the years, I can remember my mother praying out loud for God to do something about this house of ill repute. Here is what happened. As we were driving to town one day, we looked off to the side where the motel was and saw that it was terribly flooded. The strange thing was, there was no flooding anywhere else around this area, and it didn't even look like there had been a rainstorm. My mother instantly knew what had happened. She said out loud, "God flooded that place!" If your mom says God flooded it, and you're five years old, then God flooded it.

Fast-forward about thirty-one years, and I am working as a finance manager at a very old and respected furniture store. The very first day on the job, the appliance manager pulled me aside to have a private conversation about a very important customer.

"Mike, I need to make you aware of a gentleman that comes into our store frequently and buys an incredible amount of merchandise. Don't get worried about big purchases from him or the big balance he carries with us. He is good for it. He pays $2,000 a month or more without fail. The reason I am bringing this up is because he is quite a character. The truth is…well, he is a pimp. He has a place here in town and one in St. Louis. So please, for the good of the store, give him the red-carpet treatment," the appliance manager begged.

As the years went by in my position there, it was just as he described. There would be very large purchases, and of course he always paid off his account like an A credit customer. Strangely, through the years, this gentleman would sit by my desk, and I would share with him things about God. My staff thought I was crazy, but it just came natural to me and thought to myself, *Who needs a doctor? Is it the sick or the healthy?*

So one day, this pimp was sitting and rehashing his past incarcerations and gunshot wounds with me in a braggadocious manner. He had gotten his start in crime working in Waterloo where I grew up. For some reason, the motel story jumped into my mind because I knew the era he was speaking of fell close to the event of the flood.

"Do you remember the Good Times Motel there on 218?" I asked him, somewhat sheepishly.

"Why, yes, I do. I knew that place well!" he exclaimed with a little surprise in his voice.

Something in my heart always wondered if my mom was crazy about some of the things she told me as a child. I always believed her as a child. But as I got older, I started to doubt the veracity of some of these stories. I will share another story later in the book along these lines.

"Well, I have a question for you since you remember it well. Do you remember when that motel was flooded really badly back in the early seventies?"

He used a few expletives for effect and said, "Oh, yeah, I remember that. That was the craziest thing I have ever seen. It poured down rain on the place like crazy. It was like there was a single cloud just hovering over the place. There wasn't any flooding anywhere else, let alone rain. Yes, sir, that was really something. You remember that?" he questioned.

"Yes, I do. My mom prayed that rainstorm into existence. My dad was cheating on her down there, and she asked God to do something about it. He did," I confessed.

This is a perfect example of how, when we defer our problems to God rather than taking them into our own hands, He can do so much more than we could in our own strength. God is a just God. And when we pray for justice, He hears us. We have to pray with this truth in mind. There is a passage in the Bible where the person says, "Yahweh, rebuke you." This is handing off the problem and responsibility to God, just like Mom did with the motel.

CHAPTER 6

The Fish God and the Poorest in Africa

GOD IS INFINITELY intelligent. He is the repository of *everything*! When you have a question, He beats Google and Bing. He doesn't need a chord, electricity, or the Internet. He isn't artificial intelligence. He is true intelligence. His answers are without bias, and they are full of *all* context. He is the *source* of everything and the authority on every subject. I have had times in my life when I pondered things in my heart or flat out asked a question from Him, and it never fails. The answer arrives from some unsuspected place and proves every time He knows my every thought and desire. This is an intimacy some people never operate with on a daily basis. Some of us have the awareness. But then the cares of the world and all the channels make us forget this intimacy is there for us to operate in all the time. In fact, this is the intimacy He wants with us. I read somewhere that prior to 1860, most Christians stated that God spoke to them regularly.

It was a time of little interference. No radios, TVs, Internet, cell phone were present to rob our attention to Him. It was a time when His voice could be heard easily. I think we can get quiet and seclude ourselves to hear easily, but it has to be a deliberate act. God hasn't changed. We have.

So one time I was reading the Bible, and it said, "You shall not make for yourself a carved image, any likeness of anything that is in heaven above or that is in the earth beneath or that is in the water under the earth." I was walking down the street and thinking about the scripture. I couldn't think of anything that people would worship that was under the sea. I asked God, "What would someone worship beneath the sea?" No joke, my phone rang. It was a friend of mine who has an uncanny ability to get offtrack in conversation. He darts left and right in his thought process. He starts talking about random stuff that no one has any idea why he started talking about that subject. I love him dearly and try to track with him. He is an amazing musician and a sincere child of God. I think many musicians who can play without sheet music are much like this.

So he called me as I was walking down the sidewalk to get coffee, and out of the blue, he started talking about *Dagon the fish god* that the Philistines worshipped! I had read the scripture of Dagon, but I didn't know he was a likeness of a fish. Man, I was floored. As if this wasn't enough, another person I talked to later that day brought up the same Dagon and expounded on the story further.

On another occasion, I was pondering in my heart about how to help people in Africa. I was wondering where there was the greatest need. I went to bed without a clear answer.

That night, as I dreamed, I had a dream of a map. And when I woke, all I could remember from the map was the letters HAD. I pulled up a map, and right there, in the middle of the map of Africa, was the country *Chad*. I spend more time researching. I found the CIA fact list on different countries. And after reading, it was very clear that the most desperate county was in fact *Chad*. The country had been plagued with war and famine.

If you have been operating in your own intelligence or wisdom, I would challenge you to start leaning on His understanding. It is a Bible verse that most people know but don't walk it out.

> Trust in the Lord with all your heart
> and lean not on your own understand-
> ing; in all your ways submit to him,
> and he will make your paths straight.
> Do not be wise in your own eyes; fear
> the Lord and shun evil. This will bring
> health to your body and nourishment
> to your bones.

CHAPTER 7

Car Thieves Got Nothing Up on the Holy Spirit

IT'S CLEAR; GOD is on our side. If you read through the psalms and the proverbs, you find verse after verse saying how He watches over us and wants to be our protector. There are angels watching over us. There is wonderful attention paid to our lives that we barely know. I pray that God will open your eyes to His care extended over your life.

I remember when I started to hear God talk to me in the still, small voice. I was selling vacuum cleaners for the Kirby company in Kansas City. I had pulled into a gas station in my minivan. At that time, I was addicted to cigarettes, and stopping at gas stations was something I often did to get a pack or get a pop.

I got out of my van and walked to the door of the building. As I was opening the door, I heard the Holy Spirit say, "Look back!" I turned around, and to my surprise, there was a lady getting into my van, trying to steal it. I shouted, "Hey, what are you doing?"

She jumped back in the car next to my van, and they sped off in a hurry.

Years later, I was contacted by a business friend who said he had a salesperson who worked for him who needed to get a cosigner for a car loan. He was willing to pay quite a bit to someone to cosign a note for him. It was a very attractive offer. I was convinced that the financial reward was worth the risk. If I would have read my Bible closer, I would have known that was a bad idea.

I told my business friend I thought I could do the loan, but I needed to see the car he was buying. They were supposed to bring the car over the next day to my house. That night, my wife had a dream. She woke up the next morning and said, "Mike, I had a dream last night. There was this man and woman trying to get into your pocket. It was a really bad feeling I had as I watched them getting into your pocket, like they were stealing." My wife had no knowledge that I had intended to sign this loan for the couple. I had not brought it up to her, which actually wasn't intentional. God was looking out for us. I assume the couple would have defaulted, and we would have been stuck with payments we didn't need.

CHAPTER 8

Walmart Angel

RICK IS A very good friend of mine. Rick was always frugal with his money. A devoted son, Rick took care of his elderly mom, Bernice, for many years, looking after her every need.

When Rick stumbled across a Geo Metro car that would get incredible gas mileage in comparison to his Grand Marquis, it was like Rick had struck gold in the Colorado Rockies. He was tickled that he could drive so many miles on one gallon of gas, and I was happy for him. I knew they were on a fixed income, and this would help their budget.

As Rick was headed down Blairs Ferry Rd. in Cedar Rapids, he passed in front of Walmart and suddenly was hit by a driver on his driver's side door. It was a terrible accident, and Rick lay unconscious, trapped behind the wheel of this subcompact car.

Now I need to make you aware of some logistical hurdles. Rick is a very large man. He is over six feet, six inches tall and at the time weighed over four hundred pounds. Sound like a professional wrestler type? Yes, that was his job at one time.

To add context to this story, I need to explain how I know the details of this story. A lady who relayed this story and who was helpful in taking care of Rick was parked in the Walmart parking lot at the moment of the accident. She ran over to the scene and watched as a fellow who looked quite capable managed to open the door of the car. As much as he tried, he simply could not pull Rick from the wreckage of this Geo Metro.

So as his attempts failed, suddenly an elderly lady walked over to the car. She grabbed Rick up out of the car, like he was a stuffed animal, and laid him on the ground. She began lifesaving CPR, and Rick began to cough up blood. At this point, the little old lady turned to the lady from the parking lot and said very calmly, "Now, you have some towels in your car. Why don't you grab one to help wipe his face."

The lady retrieved a towel and handed it to the little old lady who carefully wiped his face.

At this point, the little lady said gently, prior to the ambulance arriving, "Well, I must be on my way now," and she walked away.

So if it isn't clear to you by now, my dear friend was saved from death by an angel. How does a little old lady lift a man of this size, pinched in behind a steering wheel out of the car when a healthy grown man failed? How did she know that the lady from Walmart had towels in her car? Why didn't she wait for the ambulance or police? Why didn't she want the news crew to interview her later? She didn't need man's accolades or notoriety. She was a messenger on a mission, and to make the most high God happy through obedience is payment enough.

Rick had a very long recovery in the years ahead. His life was tremendously changed because of his injuries, yet *he lived on*! I told you he was caring for his elderly mother who really needed him. God knew her future needs, and she was a righteous woman who Rick still claims never spoke an ill word of anyone even when it seemed it might be appropriate, if you get my drift.

Rick continues his recovery and maintains a positive attitude to this day. He can't remember much of the accident, but thanks to the woman in the parking lot. We know angels are watching over us. Praise be to God!

CHAPTER 9

Chrome Bridge

SHE INVITED ME to one of my favorite restaurants and, with a somewhat giddy manner of speech, told me she wanted a separation. This separation would ultimately end in a divorce. That week, when I found out the family was being split apart, was really hard, yet God had a plan. At the time, I was really emotional. We had tried for years to get along, but it was not meant to be.

I went to bed and woke up from a very unusual dream. I could remember the dream vividly. I was climbing something, like a chrome-plated ladder that arched out over a body of water, almost like a bridge. As I climbed the ladder, I reached the middle of the body of water, and strangely, the bridge ended there. There was no way to completely cross the body of water. The bridge was partially constructed out to that point.

I went to work that morning, pondering the unusual dream and the meaning. I knew it was a prophetic dream, which I am accustomed to having. Sometimes dreams are literal, and sometimes they are representative.

It was a Thursday morning, and I know this because we always had manager meetings on Thursday morning. I was working at a large furniture store, which was more like a department store. It had an appliance department, jewelry, flooring, and furniture, of course. As I walked into the break room that was adjacent to the large conference room where we held our manager meeting, I was greeted by Sid, who was the manager of the jewelry department.

Sid was a friend who I would discuss religious matters with from time to time. Sid was a devout Jew who taught at the local synagogue and his words are, "Jesus was a pretty smart guy." We had a lot of good talks on slow nights at the store. I would bring him coffee back from the coffee shop down the street many mornings.

On this Thursday morning, Sid had a very serious and concerned look on his face. "Mike, I heard about what's going on with your marriage. I need to tell you something. Mike, in a marriage, it's like this. Marriage is like two people building a bridge across a river. One starts on this side, and the other starts on the opposite side, and they meet in the middle to complete the bridge. Mike, you are doing your part, but she has to do hers. She may not want to do her part, and that is just how it is," he explained sincerely.

I had goose bumps from my head to my toes. I stood there speechless for a minute, trying to figure out how hours ago, I had a dream, and a jeweler just told me the interpretation of the dream with no knowledge of it. Have you ever read the story of Daniel interpreting the dream for the king who wouldn't even tell the magicians what the dream was in the first place? Think about that for a second. How can you possibly interpret a dream without first hearing the dream? I walked through this very experience. If this story doesn't impact your belief that an all-knowing God exists and actively jumps into our life when He needs or wants to show us love, then nothing will. Jesus (Yeshua) said, "If you don't believe what I say, then at least believe because of the miracles you have witnessed with your own two eyes." That is my paraphrase. This is the purpose of writing your Bible.

"Sid, you are not going to believe what I have to tell you," I said, shaking in my shoes. "Sid, just this morning, I had a dream. I was climbing this shiny ladder over a body of water, and it ended halfway out over the body of water. Sid, you just interpreted that dream for me just now. This is incredible."

Sid looked at me like he knew that he had just told me a message from God. He didn't say much at all. Additional words weren't needed. We went into the meeting, and I sat there for an hour in shock at the power of my God to know everything in my life.

He knows everything going on in your life—*everything*! This knowledge is simply life-changing at the most base level. Sit and think about this truth. Not only does He know everything but really cares to help you through your most difficult trials. Take courage, my friend. "Be strong and courageous. Do not be afraid; do not be discouraged, for the Lord your God will be with you wherever you go" are the words on my office wall compliments of my wife, Michelle.

CHAPTER 10

Imaginary Government

You may know a person close to you who deals with a mental illness or possibly demonic attacks. It's hard to know what is really going on in the mind of people who are troubled. And with respect for the mental health professionals, I can say with certainty that sometimes issues are spiritually oriented and not chemical in nature.

I grew up with one such person, who was a dear friend. He had struggled for more than thirty years being diagnosed as bipolar. Through the years, we would get together to have coffee and discuss life. I would encourage him to write and encourage him that there was greatness in him. We would debate religion many times. He went through many phases, exploring different faiths and rationalizing away the existence of God in some cases.

Through the years, his poor choices in times of a bipolar manic high or depression led to abandonment by almost all his close friends and family. There is a lot of collateral damage when you get close to someone like this, and it is not for the faint of heart. In all honesty, it was challenging to continue my friendship at times as things were just too chaotic to have to be in his life. I had to draw some boundaries while trying to continue offering unconditional love in the spirit of doing my best to reflect Yeshua living in me.

No greater love has a man that he would lay down his life for his friend are the words of Yeshua. One year I felt a compulsion to begin a fast of sorts. I didn't realize it at the time I started to fast, but the day I began was forty days before Yom Kippur, which is a traditional time of fasting and reflecting in Jewish culture and is a biblical tradition.

My fast wasn't as hard as some fasts that people do. I had a milkshake every day that I made with ice cream, peanut butter, and bananas. It was a bunch of calories to be sure, and I didn't start to lose any weight for at least a week. That was my meal each day for forty days. And I can tell you, after a while, the smell of the meals my family was eating was like torture. I would have gladly traded my shake for a steak or spaghetti.

My fast was closely tied to my friend who I had prayed for so many years. I wanted him to know God and to understand His love for him. I prayed fervently during this fast that he would be saved. I didn't really talk to him much during the fast, but he did know I was doing a fast.

At the conclusion of the fast, I made a trek to my hometown, Waterloo. He and I got together for coffee. I was in for a big surprise. As we talked, he opened up to me. "Mike, there's something I need to tell you. You know how I go into my fantasy world about the government?" he asked me.

My friend had shared with me how he would imagine different positions of the federal government and would make up names and stories around these characters. It was a fantasy world that he created and escaped from reality into each day.

"Mike, my fantasy world had been getting completely out of control. I was spending four and five hours a day completely lost in this fantasy, completely out of touch with reality. It was getting out of control, and I didn't know how to stop. This is a pretty big deal what I am going to tell you. When you stopped fasting, the need to fantasize stopped for me. I really can't explain that, and I guess I am saying, I am more convinced or curious than I have ever been," he confessed in an earnest voice.

I was unaware that his problem was that severe. He had never told me the extent to which this fantasy world had gone for him. I was so happy for him, and he started to attend church for some time. He made some friends, and they seemed to encourage him like I did. I can't say that his life looked like he accepted Yeshua as his Savior in the years that led up to his death.

His life tragically ended some years later in a hotel-makeshift apartment complex where he passed away from a deadly cocktail of pills and alcohol. I was very, very sad that his life had to end this way and prayed to God. "Lord, all of that time and effort to bring him to you, and here it ends like this. It was all for nothing," I said selfishly.

Suddenly I heard such a sweet message float into my mind that I will never forget. "Yes, but then again, there is grace," he said.

I don't think we can fathom truly the grace of our Father. Things may appear one way to us, but only God sees the heart of man. I have since contemplated the fact that my friend spent more time than many people trying hard to find the *real* God. Seek, and you will find. Knock, and the door will be opened. I think the door opened. And even though it looked like it closed, it never did.

CHAPTER 11

Baby's Name

THE SWEETEST THING a man can experience is a little, tiny kick in the back as his wife lies next to him. I really don't remember how far along she was into the pregnancy, but I do remember the most incredible baby name for us.

I awoke to that little nudge on my spine. The lucent curtains refracted the sun's rays. I woke and struggled as I wanted to wake her but knew she was sleeping soundly. The thought jumped into my mind as to what I should name our baby. I said in my mind, "Lord, what is this baby's name?"

Immediately, I heard Him say, "Samuel."

A week had gone by, and I was driving back from the store to our home on Ozark Street. I pulled in, and shortly, our friends, Fred and Jenny, pulled up in this cool half motorcycle, half moped. I invited them to the backyard, where we had a firepit started.

As we visited, our friends asked if we knew what the gender was of the new baby. I told them it was a baby boy but that we hadn't decided on a name yet. I was still pondering the name God had said, almost doubting Him.

My friend Fred looked up with a thoughtful expression and said very slowly, "Samuel."

I looked at him, realizing that this was a small miracle of God's intervention. I said, "Yes, yes, that is his name." I went on to tell them how God had told me earlier that week what his name was and how I was doubting. It wasn't my choice, but it was His choice, and that made me so happy!

I realize now that God knows us in the womb. What is most important to me, and maybe to you, is that God sees us as a person even before we are born. He has a name for us. He knows our future and what we will be like in the future. He has a magnificent plan for us. It makes me so happy for all moms throughout the world!

CHAPTER 12

Let It Rain

WITH THE ADVENT of social media and the Internet, the world has become smaller. We can meet and interact with people in different countries and cultures easily.

Many years ago, I became acquainted with a gentleman through Facebook, who has an orphanage in India. His name is Joseph. After talking with Joseph for many months and helping him out financially with the kids, I was presented with a different need by Joseph.

At the time, we were refinishing our wood floors in our modest home on Ozark and literally had our living room sofa sitting in the kitchen. It was quite crowded, as you can imagine. Morgan, my daughter, and I were talking to Joseph on video when he started to explain how bad things were in his part of the world. "It has not rained here in months, sir! We are in desperate need of water."

For some reason, on that day and at that moment, my faith became as big as a mountain. I really don't know why. I am just an ordinary person who has doubts and fears. But on that day, something was special. I spoke boldly to Joseph, "Well, it's going to rain now. You watch and see, Joseph. We are going to pray together, and it's going to rain. Heavenly Father, you know our needs before we even tell you. Right now, this part of India where Joseph lives is in desperate need of rain. I know you care about your children and even the animals in this area, Lord, and so ask that you bring the rain. Amen."

The next day, Joseph called me with such joy in his voice, "Sir, it is raining as you said! Praise be to Jesus!" He was smiling from ear to ear. I smiled and cried because that's just how I am. He did it. He came through in a pinch, just like He always does.

In recent months, I have rejoiced over the abundance of rain God has poured over the Western United States. There have been bad consequences of mudslides and physical damage, but at the same time, the West was in desperate need of rain. I know I am not the only one who has prayed that the water supply would be restored there, with so many lives at stake.

I wrote a post on Facebook the other day that said, "Can we stop hating on precipitation?" Our news sources always seem to demonize rain and snow when in fact we need these things for survival. And the truth is, the Bible describes rain as a blessing, not a curse.

CHAPTER 13

Michelle

IN 2004, I became an eligible bachelor. I had been married for eleven years, and I had five beautiful daughters. This was a new beginning, and it was exciting yet a little frightening to go back to a point where I would need to find a wife.

I made up my mind that I was going to do things differently than I did in the past as a young adult. My teenage years and early twenties were a time when I was definitely not a good example of how to live. I was very promiscuous and lived a very wild lifestyle. I am not proud of how I lived. So at the point of starting over, I made a decision that I would court rather than date my new bride.

Courting is different from dating in that from the very start of the relationship, you are intending to be married to the person. The decision to marry has been established rather than the mindset of dating, where there is a try-it-out philosophy involved between the two people. The courting process can be short or long, but simply you are headed toward marriage for sure.

I met a young woman at church, and she had a son. She was a very godly person and seemed like a person who was on fire for the Lord. I spent some time around her in group settings and thought, *Well, maybe this is the one.*

For several Sundays, when I was at church, I kept hearing God tell me to invite this couple, who taught at my daughter Amadea's Sunday school class, over to my house. It seemed so awkward. I couldn't do it. I am not a shy person, but I just couldn't work up the nerve to ask them over. I didn't know them.

So after a couple Sundays of having God say this, I was at Noelridge Park with two of my daughters, Jerri Dale and Amadea. They wanted to go down and walk in the trickling stream that runs through the park. I said, "Go ahead."

As I followed them upstream, as I was looking at my little Gideon pocket Bible, some lady, who seemed annoyed, yelled over to me, "Are those your kids?" as she walked around the walking trail.

As I turned to answer her, the couple who taught Amadea's class came around the corner on the same trail. At that moment, I said to God, "Okay, I give up. You win." I walked over to them and said, "Hey, aren't you Amadea's teachers?" sounding pretty dumb.

They smiled and said, "Yes, we are. We live right over there," as they motioned toward the neighborhood just east of the park.

I said, "Are you going to the playground?" and learned they were.

So my daughters and I hung out with them for a bit at the park, and then I dropped the question, "How would you like to come over to my house for a God party?" I had been having God parties at my house where we played loud music, worshipped, and stayed up too late.

"Sure, that sounds like fun," they said as they giggled.

I gave them my address and walked home with my girls.

About thirty minutes passed, and they pulled up out front. Then another vehicle pulled up. Tiffany, who was the wife, came up to the door and said, "We invited Jim's sister over too. I hope that's okay."

"Sure, that's great," I answered her with a smile. We all went to the backyard, where the kids played.

Jim's sister, Michelle, did cartwheels with the kids and played with them on the swing set.

About a half hour later, the girl I thought might be my new wife showed up. She visited with everyone, and we had a really good time talking and getting to know each other. Jim and Tiffany were new believers, and they were really on fire to evangelize others. In fact, Michelle had really become serious about her faith as a result of Jim and Tiffany.

Shortly after this God party, I proposed. She said no after she prayed about it. We stayed friends. And because I didn't behave like I did years ago, this friendship exists to this day. I am thankful that she was a person who sought guidance from God.

So a little time passed, and it was getting tough. I was not used to being single. I called my friend and told him as I was driving to the prayer center, "Hey, man, I need you to pray for me. I am just not wired like this. I need a wife, and I need one soon."

We prayed together, and he assured me things would work out.

The following day, I had to go to small claims court. Working as a finance manager meant that sometimes we would have to sue for a money judgment against people who do not pay. I was sitting on the third floor of the Linn County Courthouse next to one of my credit associates, Lisa.

"I don't know why, but I am pretty certain that I am going to be married again by the end of the year," I confessed to Lisa.

Just then, around the corner walked this girl that had come to my house for the God party. It was Jim's sister.

"Hey, I know her. That girl just came over to my house the other day. That's funny," I explained to Lisa.

I walked over to Michelle and said, "Weren't you just over to my house the other day?" I questioned her.

"Yes," she said bashfully. She was very quiet and soft-spoken.

"Well, it was nice to see you," I said as I walked back to my bench.

What I didn't know until weeks later was that God had told Michelle she was going to see me downtown that very day. What Michelle didn't know was that right before she walked around the corner, I had said I was going to get married this year. Just wait; it gets better.

I became friends with Jim's nephew, who was a young teenager that lived a couple of blocks from our house. He was a new Christian and seemed like a good kid but had been in some trouble. We hung out and talked about God for a period of time. One time I heard the nephew talking to his mom about Michelle. He got off the phone, and I asked, "Is everything okay with Michelle?"

"Well, she is out of food or something," He told me.

"Well, she can't go without food! That's crazy. She has three little kids. Get in the van," I commanded.

We went to Walmart, and I bought a cart full of groceries. We headed for her apartment. As we arrived, he ran to the apartment to announce we were there. He returned to the car with a weird look on his face. "Uh, Mike, I guess I kind of made a mistake. She actually has plenty of groceries. I'm sorry," he lamented.

"Well, we brought them here, and they aren't going back to my place," I said firmly. My girls were only with me every other weekend during that particular six months of the year, and there was no way I could eat up everything I had purchased. So we carried in groceries as these little three-year-old boys ran around like madmen. They were so full of energy and cute as could be. There was her little nine-month-old girl in the car seat, sucking a bottle down. Michelle thanked me, and we said goodbye.

Here is a little foreshadowing: About a month or two before meeting Michelle, I had borrowed a book called *Bringing Up Boys* by Dr. James Dobson. What is funny is that at the time, I had no sons. I had heard Dobson talk about the book so much that when I saw Rebecca had a copy, I asked to borrow it. As I was starting to read this book alone at my house one afternoon, I read this part where these twin boys, who were three years old, stuck beans up their noses. If you have never had a Holy Spirit–filled laughter, you will not understand this. I laughed so hard when

I read the story of these two boys. But as I laughed, it was this strange, wholesome feeling that I was enraptured by. I laughed at my laughter. My all-alone laughing moment was prophetic, but I didn't know it at the time. Soon I would be fathering twin three-year-old boys.

Jim and Tiffany called me and invited me to their house for a cookout. I took them up on the offer. On my way to their house, I stopped at the store. Across, in the next checkout, was Michelle. She was there buying stuff for the cookout too. We had a great time that day. And as I reflected later, it seemed odd how I kept running into her.

I called Michelle from work and asked if she was going to church that Wednesday evening. She said yes and told me which class she attended. I told her I would go to that class also. That night, Michelle gave me a letter. She told me to read it later. In my mind, I was thinking, *Oh, here we go. This is one of those "I like you, do you like me" letters right out of a country western song.* Nope, I was wrong. In the letter, Michelle told me how blessed I was by God and in so many words encouraged me to keep on being the man I am. I was a little shocked and embarrassed at my immaturity.

Michelle and I started hanging out at my house, talking about God, reading some of my poems, and really learning about each other. After a while, we both started to think, maybe we were meant for each other, given how things had unfolded and the meeting at the courthouse. I explained to Michelle that I was not going to date but only court.

Michelle called me one day at work, and we started talking about whether we should court. I told Michelle, I thought maybe I should fleece God.

If you are unfamiliar with fleecing, I will explain briefly. In the Bible, Gideon was trying to figure out if God wanted him and his army to go to war. He asked God to put dew on top of fleece and not on the ground around it as a sign that he should go to war. Then, after God answered the fleece in almost-comical fashion, he asked God to reverse the results, just to be sure. I am smiling as I write this because I doubt like this too, as you will discover later. So God answered again in the affirmative, and Gideon was off to war.

So I explained this to Michelle over the phone, and she said, "Well, I will do a fleece as well."

We hung up the phone. I ripped a piece of paper off my adding machine and wrote down the oddest, most random thing which popped into my mind. It was the words "Red china for the kitchen." I took the paper, put it in an envelope, and handed it to my assistant manager, telling her to keep it in her desk drawer. I guess this made it more official. I am laughing again.

The next thing I knew, Michelle invited me to her mom's house for a cookout. We drove out to her acreage near Mt. Vernon. It was a pretty place with horses and lots of big oak trees. We walked in off the back deck into the living room. Immediately, like a magnet, my eyes were fixed on the corner shelf that had all this beautiful red glassware. I walked over without saying a word. I looked at it closely, and there was a little boy and girl who were obviously in love on the glassware. I just stared at it without saying a word. Dianna, Michelle's mom, came over to me and started talking. "Oh, do you like this? It's quite beautiful, isn't it? That piece you're looking at was purchased down at Smulekoff's where you work, in the china department. Doug and I have been thinking about selling this set because we would rather have the money," she explained. It was like she was trying to sell me the china, and I just met her. It was from the place I worked. It had two people in love painted on it. What on earth could be going on? I was in a trance for a few minutes, completely floored.

We left the house. And as Michelle drove the gravel road, I confessed. "Michelle, I have to tell you something. I am pretty sure God just answered my fleece. As strange as it may sound, my fleece was red china for the kitchen. I can show you the piece of paper I wrote it on. It was the first thing that popped into my mind when we hung up the phone that day," I explained.

Michelle smiled and started to laugh as she said, "What is so funny is that she was trying to sell that glassware to get money to help me out financially."

About a week later, I had to go to New York for training. While I was there, I attended a fancy dinner sponsored by a software company. It was a dinner theater performance, and the play was called *Tony and Tina's Wedding*.

Michelle had offered to watch my house while I was gone that week. When I got back home, she picked me up at the airport in my van. As we loaded my luggage, Michelle said, "God answered my fleece." We got in the van.

"What was it?" I asked.

"Apple pie," she said happily. "Your daughter Alex came up to me at church this morning and asked me if I wanted to buy an apple pie for her fundraiser. So what do we do?" she asked meekly.

"I guess we get married," I said sheepishly and sort of afraid. I couldn't say it to her, but I was thinking, *Apple pie? Really? Seriously? You couldn't come with anything better than that? That's too easy! That could have popped up in a million different ways. The odds are too easy. This is a big deal. This is the rest of our life!*

Later we were back at my house, lying on the couch, watching a Rich Mullins DVD. As we lay there, she didn't know it, but I was pouring out my heart to God, "God this is a big deal. I don't think she is my type. She is so different than me. We just met. I hardly know her. This is a forever thing. It's a huge step. Her fleece was so easy."

Boom! A flash of memory! Lightning bolt! Suddenly I remembered something from about two months earlier. I was walking through the Walmart frozen foods section with the friend named Rebecca, who I thought might be the one. As I started to say something to her, I tried to say Rebecca, but the name Michelle came flying off my tongue. I was so embarrassed because I called her by some other person's name. I nervously just kept walking, never acknowledging my mistake. I didn't know a Michelle at the time whom I interacted with regularly. I was thinking, *How could I do that?* Now I understand. God knew way in advance. How incredible that this happened but even more incredible that He could cause the memory to pop into my brain as I questioned this marriage.

I jumped off the couch and shouted, "Michelle, you are never going to believe this! I was just lying here, telling God all this stuff, doubting whether we should get married, and He shoved this memory to the forefront of my brain from when I was walking through the store with Rebecca. And I called her Michelle out of the blue! Oh my gosh. Oh man. Okay, I'm good now. I know that I know that I know you are the one. I feel so much peace now."

Michelle had known for a while. When she first came to my house, she said God had told her it was going to be her home. She didn't tell me until everything was done. We got married. And since then, we have had eleven additional children. Five of our children were born at home with just Michelle, myself, and the angels present at the time of birth.

So much of God's handiwork can only be recognized in retrospect. He is painting a beautiful portrait in our life. Many times, we can only see one brushstroke in a day or a week. It's important to record daily events and to pay attention so you can write your Bible later.

For Michelle and me, our marriage has been so sturdy through tough times because we both know it was a marriage orchestrated by God that we entered into because of Him and not just because of our own fleshly desires.

My wife is a very beautiful person inside and out. She is a great mom and a wonderful best friend. I am so eternally grateful to God for such a great gift.

He knows what He is doing, so I encourage you to listen to Him when it comes to relationships. Throw out your preconceived notions, and lean on His understanding. He knows the heart of all who live. Who could be better equipped to join two souls together?

CHAPTER 14

Cattle Congress Midway

Every year, the town of Waterloo, Iowa, holds a cattle competition, along with concerts and carnival that is embedded in every person's memory for the past seventy-five years who lived in Waterloo. I was fortunate to live right beside the railroad tracks that would bring the Barnum & Bailey Circus to town. I could see beneath the railroad cars the long, fat legs of elephants headed for the hippodrome. What a sight it was for a young lad who may never get to see them live in the stadium.

Prior to living by the tracks, my mom encountered a very unusual encounter with God that involved Cattle Congress. My mom was at home on the farm by La Porte when all of a sudden, an open-eyed vision unfolded before her. It was as if someone pulled a curtain back on an old-time theater. What she saw was not good. She saw a woman walking hand in hand with my dad as they walked through the Cattle Congress midway, where all of the carnival rides were placed. I don't remember exactly what my mom said, but it was something like, "She was a blonde-haired lady, wearing a red dress."

When my dad arrived home that night, my mom approached him with great confidence, considering my dad had been violent with her before. She said firmly, "So who was the blonde you were walking through the midway with at Cattle Congress, wearing the red dress?"

My dad stood there, shocked for a moment, realizing that my mom had been following him but not exactly as he anticipated. "What were you doing following me around Cattle Congress?" He tried putting her on the defense.

"I wasn't following you around, Gerald. God showed me in a vision what you were up to today," she exclaimed.

My dad was speechless. And because she brought God into the situation, there was little he could say.

You see, even people who are doing things that are sinful are helpless when you introduce an all-powerful God into the situation. We should never be afraid.

This story reminds me of a little old lady that was accosted by a robber, who had every intention of stealing from her and leaving her for dead. She began to witness him. And soon he surrendered his gun and changed his life by going the straight and narrow path.

God is hope. God is protection. God is the way out of impossible circumstances. God is just. These are always truthful proverbs.

CHAPTER 15

Prophetic Novel

In 2006, I left work as a finance manager and started a career in fire safety, selling smoke detectors and other lifesaving equipment. During this time, I began writing a novel that I intend to publish soon called, "The Elijah Test." I will try not to spoil the chance to enjoy the other book by talking about too many details.

So during my first months selling smoke detectors, I had the chance to work with a gentleman, who was quite a bit older, by the name of John. John lived in a small town called Baxter, which is pretty close to Des Moines, Iowa. During my time working with John, He was kind enough to invite me into his home for a couple nights while we worked together.

One morning, I remember waking up, and his wife, Connie, was cooking, and John was watching TV. He was watching this nun talking on a Catholic station, and he said to me with a chuckle, "I get the biggest kick out of Sister Frangelica. She is a hoot!"

I didn't know Sister Frangelica, and I just accepted that she must be fun to listen to based on his experience. So from that point forward, I knew John and Connie were Catholic. We didn't really talk about religion a lot, but I knew John believed in God. And of course, I knew he was German because that was talked about often.

That morning, we went out past a small cemetery in John's big Lincoln Town Car. He drove past the cemetery and then proceeded to tell me about people he knew that were buried there as he backed up the car at a slow pace. I knew I was experiencing something spiritual but couldn't tell what it was for sure. I just had an unusual feeling, like God was showing me something significant.

The next week, as I was writing my new novel, I chose Baxter as a town to be where a grandpa, named Keezie, lived in my story. I used my real-life experience in small ways to write a fictional account. One of the subthemes of the novel is that there are thousands of Hebrews or Jews living in the Midwest, whose ancestors escaped persecution by fleeing to the United States and taking on the cover of being a good Catholic, Lutheran, or some other protestant faith to avoid further persecution. So many people are unaware that there have been recorded over a thousand events in Europe and Russia of systematic persecution against Jewish people in the past two thousand years. Sadly, many times, these attacks were in the name of Jesus. I know my Savior does not approve since He is the Lion of the tribe of Judah.

So I finished the novel in 2006 in record time but was too afraid to publish it because I feared some weirdo might attack my family or me for the controversial nature of the story. I have gotten past that fear and intend to publish it this year.

Fast-forward to 2018, and I am working in an entirely different line of work, selling energy-saving products, like reflective insulation and solar-powered attic fans. Strangely, the fellow mentioned from the fire alarm business was now working for the same company as well. He was a manager of the warehouse in Des Moines, where I would routinely pick up insulation. That afforded me many chances to sit and visit with John. We were friends that talked on the phone, but it was better when we could talk in person.

On one of my last visits to the warehouse before John retired, we were just shooting the breeze, and John was expounding on his years-of-business wisdom. I tend to be a good student of seniors. They have been around the block and made mistakes that can profoundly save us from stupid decisions if we will just listen. John finished up a statement. And in a self-deprecating manner, he said, "Well, heck, what do I know? I'm just an old German Jew!"

What? Wait a second What did he just say? I thought I heard something wrong. "Hey, John, would you like to have lunch?" I inquired.

"Sure, why not," he said easily.

We got seats in some Mexican place close to the office. We talked for a bit, and then I had to ask. "Hey, John, you remember when we were back at the warehouse, you said something about being an old German Jew. What were you trying to say?" I queried softly.

"Well, I am. I thought you knew that. Didn't you know that?" he said in a shocked tone of voice.

I started laughing. "I know this is stupid, but I always thought you were Catholic because you were watching that Sister Frangelica that you said was such a hoot way back when I stayed with you that time. Clearly, my assumption was wrong," I confessed.

"Mike, let me tell you something. You know I was raised right there in that town of Baxter where you stayed. That entire town was Jewish folks when I was a boy. The only guy who wasn't a Jew was the butcher that I worked for there as a young man. Most people in town were not very nice to him, but I was," John explained.

"Wait a minute! *You have got to be kidding me*! You are telling me the whole town was a bunch of Jewish people? John, I have goose bumps all over my body. This is incredible. John, I knew nothing about the town or its history! Do you remember me telling you about the book where I used my time in Baxter with you as part of my fictional book I wrote? John, in my book, Keezie is a Jew, and I had no idea you were a Jew, let alone the whole town. And I don't know if you remember when we went to the cemetery. But when you drove past it and started backing up, and for some reason, it reminded me of how, in Hebrew, you read from right to left. I wrote that book not even knowing that God was orchestrating the storyline, it seems."

The Holy Spirit does guide us especially when doing something in service of God.

CHAPTER 16

Broken Pipes in Florida

WE RECENTLY OPENED a new office for our company, Energy Nerds, in Ft. Myers, Florida. We had experienced a terrible hurricane called a derecho in my own town of Cedar Rapids just a couple of years ago. The storm resulted in our company purchasing many vacuums that remove insulation. They are quite expensive items. We had been planning to open another office but never thought about Florida since our first two offices were in the Midwest. When Hurricane Ian happened in 2022, someone in our company suggested we open up an office in Florida. After thinking about it and traveling to Florida to assess the damage, we decided to open the office. We already had most of the expensive equipment, and it was sitting around, doing nothing.

One thing we didn't see coming when it came to Florida attics was the pipes in the attics. Nearly every house has pipes in the attic, and many of these pipes are quite brittle. PVC sitting at 150 degrees gets sensitive to the touch, it seems.

One of our very first removals for a very sweet elderly couple resulted in a pipe break. It flooded the ceiling before they could get the water turned off and caused a lot of damage. What a mess. I felt terrible because the couple who owned the house were such nice people and felt like we made matters worse for them when they were just trying to recover from the storm.

We got the attic and downstairs dried out with fans and dehumidifiers. That was the first step. But then it was necessary to actually fix the drywall and paint the ceilings. I started calling drywall companies. Oh, boy, this was so disheartening. I called over five different places in the vicinity of their house. All of them had messages, saying things like, "We are not accepting any new clients," or "We are not taking any more messages at this time." These companies were so inundated with the influx of business caused by the hurricane; they just couldn't take on any new business. I was just beside myself.

Suddenly a thought popped into my mind. *Maybe Joe, back in Iowa, might know someone down in Florida who does drywall.* Joe was a drywaller who had worked on my own house after we had a small disaster involving an overflowed toilet. He lived in Iowa, but I remembered him saying he wanted to start a fishing excursion business in Florida sometime soon.

"Joe, this is Mike Temple. Hey, I was wondering if you might know a drywaller in Florida? I remembered you talking about Florida that one time," I asked him over the phone.

"I am in Florida right now, Mike," he shared, to my surprise.

"You're working in Florida? We opened an office in Ft. Myers, and we had a water pipe break, and we have to fix a ceiling," I explained.

"Well, I'm in Punta Gorda right now, working," he said.

"That's incredible. You're right next to where we need this job done. Do you think you could help us out? I know you've probably booked way out," I asked, thinking it would be months.

"We can work it in soon," he said very calmly.

"Joe, if you were here, I would hug you! You have no idea how much I appreciate this," I said, almost crying.

The bottom line here is, Joe went out the next day and, a week later, took care of the ceiling for these really nice people. It was looking like I was not going to be able to fix this for them for months, if not longer, and it got done a week later. Thanks to my Heavenly Father. All things work together for those who will put their trust in Him. This is not coincidence or good timing. *I called a drywaller in Iowa who was in Florida* right next to the customer *I needed to help.*

When I told the customer about what happened, she said something like, "It seems like you live a very blessed life."

I said, "Indeed I do. You are very right about that!" I gave all the credit to the Lord because I saw His fingerprints in all this situation. It gets easier and easier to see.

CHAPTER 17

Hatchet Tornado

As ANY IOWAN can tell you, tornadoes are part of life, and it can be quite frightening when the sirens go announcing impending doom. Well, it is one thing to have a tornado approaching when you are at home, but it is quite different to experience a tornado when you are camping.

One year, my family was celebrating Sukkot at the same campground by Newton, Iowa, where we drove home with an empty tank. Many people camping with us were in tents; however, we were in a cabin. However, a cabin with no basement is not going to help anyone in a tornado.

When the sirens went off, we quickly headed to the main lodge, which did have a basement. After we arrived at the lodge and got all the kids safely inside, I went upstairs to what you might call a large cement patio that overlooked a very large open field where no one had set up tents.

The field was empty, except for one man who was standing out in the middle, whom I did not know. It was curious to me to see him standing out there by himself, doing nothing, it seemed. He had a hat on that looked like an Indiana Jones hat, if you recall the movie. I watched with amazement as it seemed he was talking to the sky or praying out loud to God. Then all of a sudden, I watched as he took a hatchet that I didn't know he had, and he flung it forward with great force. The hatchet stuck in the ground perfectly.

Now if you have never heard of spiritual actions affecting the physical world, you will find this pretty amazing, just as I did. After watching this man throwing this hatchet, I returned inside. I walked downstairs to find my wife talking on the phone.

"Who are you talking to?" I asked her.

"It's Laura. She's looking at the radar. She's at home in Cedar Rapids," Michelle replied.

"Put it on speaker," I said. "Where is it, Laura?" I asked in regard to the place of the tornado.

"Well, it's really not possible for me to say where the tornado is exactly, but the whole storm front that was headed toward you has just split into two parts. One part is to the North and one to the South. So you guys are in the clear now," Laura consoled us.

"You are not going to believe what I just saw!" I said in amazement. "This guy was out in the field beside this building, and he prayed and threw this hatchet at the ground. And now you're telling me that the storm has been split apart."

It would be incorrect to say we were a little scared that day. We didn't have much shelter to take from the impending storm. In life, when we feel unprotected, we need to remember that our Heavenly Father can dismantle any storm we face. It is often quoted that Yeshua spoke to the storm, and it was still. I think life would be so much more peaceful for many of us if we really understood that He is in charge of everything, including nasty storms. I read a quote that 85 percent of worries never actually come to fruition. I would say that even the 15 percent that are legitimate can be overcome by believing in His Excellency to handle the situation. Even if the storm is real, He can cleave that problem in half.

CHAPTER 18

Self-Dialing Phone

"MIKE, YOUR NEPHEW is calling my phone. I assume he is trying to reach you. I just saw a missed call from his phone number," my older brother, Gary, yelled from the basement.

Gary had been in prison for a number of years and had been recently released to my house to live a period of time before going out on his own. Gary had called me recently when I visited my nephew in Kansas City, so he had the number saved in his phone, which is how he knew who was calling.

I picked up my phone and called to reach back out to my nephew.

"Hello," my niece Susan answered.

"Hi, Susan, I saw Richard called my brother Gary's phone just a little bit ago. Is he there."

"Yes, let me get him for you," she said.

"Hello, this Richard," he said, not knowing who was calling.

"Richard, it's Mike. I was just calling you back," I said quickly.

"Um, not sure what you are talking about. I never called, but I have some company here at the house, and I can call you back in a little bit," he said in a courteous way.

"Oh, okay, that sounds good. I just wait to hear back from you," I said in an apologetic way.

An hour went by, and he never called me back. I waited another half hour, and he never called me back. I thought, maybe he forgot to call me back. So I picked up the phone and called again. Susan answered.

"Hey, Susan, I have been waiting for Richard to call me back. Is he there?"

A long pause ensued.

"No, he's gone again. He left with a buddy. They went to the bar. He is rarely home at night," she lamented.

"Oh, oh, I see. I'm sorry to hear that, Susan. How are you doing?" I inquired.

"You know, not good, Michael. I don't know if I can hold on any longer. Nothing is changing. I have prayed and prayed, and nothing seems to get better. In fact, this morning I was standing in my kitchen, and I told God, 'You just don't listen to me!'" she said candidly.

At that moment, I could connect the dots. It was like it all made sense now. Richard didn't dial the phone; God did! Susan needed to know that God was listening, and He knew I would encourage her.

"Susan, I want to tell you something. My brother's phone rang an hour and half ago with a call from your number. Richard said he didn't call. Obviously, he was with a buddy there at your house, and so why would he? Susan, God is listening. He knows that you are trying. He knows you are a great wife and that you are putting the best effort in that anyone could possibly do. He called my phone so you could hear the truth and worked a miracle so you would see He is real and involved. Don't give up hope. I know it's hard, and I know you love him," I said confidently.

The years went by, and Susan hung in there, like an amazing warrior of God. She kept loving Richard, and eventually something happened. Richard went to the doctor, and he said, "If you don't stop drinking, you are going to die." This really grabbed Richard and took him back a step.

Here is the happy ending, and I can say I have never been as proud of someone as I am of my nephew. He turned it all around with God's help. He started attending an Alcoholics Anonymous program and eventually started a new group at his church. He has led many people to the Lord, occasionally preaches, takes wonderful care of his wife, and has raised his son to be a mighty man of God. He is devoted to helping others who struggled with alcohol and drugs with no condemnation in his heart. He shares his testimony, and the tears roll in such a beautiful, humble way. He is a changed man.

CHAPTER 19

Rapid City

"MIKE, THE COMPANY has a promotion to offer you, if you want to take it," Bob said to me. Bob was my manager at Beneficial Finance in Gladstone, Missouri. Gladstone is in the north part of Kansas City. "There is a new vanguard office in Rapid City, South Dakota, that has an opening for a manager. The only stipulation is that you have to give them an answer in the next twenty-four hours. The guy that had the position was involved in a drunk-driving accident, and they really need someone up there quick. They have been having to fly subs into the office to work for a week at a time," he explained.

"Wow. Well, that is great and sad at the same time. I have no clue where Rapid City is, Bob," I confessed "It's where Mt. Rushmore is located. Didn't you ever go there as a kid?" Bob asked with a shocked tone.

That evening, I went to the library to research Rapid City. This was just before the Internet emerged, so the library was my only option for investigating, moving to a town I had never been before. At the library, I looked at some newspaper stories on microfiche. I read what was in the encyclopedia. Frankly, the town didn't seem like such a great place to live from what I can find out.

That evening, I left the library in quite a bit of doubt about the job offer. It was a lot of pressure to make a decision in just twenty-four hours with hardly any way of knowing what it would be like to live there.

I came home and got my daughters, Taylor and Alexandria, ready for bed. I knelt down beside their bunk bed and prayed. I prayed for many of the normal things we pray for each day. But at the end, I put in my special request.

"Lord, I have this job offer, and I really don't know whether to take it or not. I don't know anything about this city, and I really need an answer from you on what to do, and I need it quickly. Amen," I finished. Dalaling, our old-fashioned landline phone, started ringing before I could get off my knees. Rushing to the phone, I said, "Hello."

"Hi, Mike there."

"Yes, this is Mike," I said.

"Hey, Mike, this is a voice from your past. Do you recognize who I am?" he said playfully.

"Uh, no, no, I really don't know who this is," I replied.

"Okay, well, I will give you a hint. Your sister, Sandy," he said.

I thought for a while, and I still couldn't make a connection. "I'm sorry. You have me stumped. I really can't think of who you might be," I said.

"Okay, here is another clue: football," he said with a giggle in his voice.

It only took me a second, and I knew. "Chewy! That's who you are!" I said, like a guy who won Jeopardy.

"Yes, that's right. But I go by David now that I am grown up. How are you, man? We haven't talked in like twenty years. Your sister told me you were living in Kansas City, and I just moved here, so I thought I would look you up and see if we can get together," Chewy explained.

"Oh, wow, that's awesome!" I said in an excited voice.

We talked for a little bit about where he worked in his career. I filled him in on what I had been doing for a career. Then after we caught up, I said, "You know, it's funny that you just moved, and I might actually be moving myself. I have a job offer and have to let them know tomorrow whether I want to take it. It's in Rapid City, South Dakota."

"*Rapid*! Oh man, Mike, I love Rapid City. I went to school up there for four years. You are going to love it. I plan to move back there someday when I retire. It is beautiful, and the people are really friendly," he excitedly told me.

"What? You lived there? Man, that is crazy! I can hardly believe this. I have to tell you, I was just praying with my girls, and I told God I need help making the decision on this offer, and I need to know fast. And as soon as I said amen, the phone rang. This is incredible! God is good, man! All the stuff at the library was pretty negative about the town, and now I have a firsthand witness from you that it is a great place to live," I confessed.

"Wow, that is cool, man. I am happy for you that you got the offer. I know you will like it up there," he assured me.

I never did get to see David before I had to go to Rapid. I ended up back in Iowa a year after moving to Rapid City. But while I was there, it was truly a very nice place to live. The mountains were beautiful. And he was right, the people were super friendly.

I have told many people that I see God's character as being a "just in time" God. He came through for me just in time. So if you think, maybe He isn't going to respond or that He isn't listening, just remember that He always comes through at exactly the right time.

CHAPTER 20

Beginning Your Bible

I HOPE YOU have enjoyed reading about God's intervention in my life and the close friends and family around me. It is my hope these stories will draw you closer to Him and, if you don't know Him, actually bring you to an understanding that He is real and wants to have a relationship with you. He is not far away.

One time, I had a dream that I was standing up in front of a crowd of people at a church, and I was teaching. I pointed to a ring I had on my index finger and said to the crowd, "God is as close to you as this ring is close to me." He is present in your day. He is present in your thoughts.

The earlier pages of this book have been about my life and my Bible, but the rest of this book is about your life and your Bible. I want to relate tangible practices that help you put this Bible together. The truth is, this Bible you write never stops until the day you pass to the other side. It can be a tremendous story and will really depend on the amount of effort you put into it. I can't wait to read your Bible! I can't wait to hear the stories of the lives impacted by all these Bibles floating across the Internet, getting printed, being talked about in social circles. It is going to be amazing! It is going to make our Heavenly Father smile from ear to ear! I know this can be part of a new revelation for our time. And if you recall, it was written about Yeshua that if the stories of His works were recorded, it would take up all the books in the world.

So let's get started. I challenge you to get a notepad or open a computer and start jotting down all the instances you can remember where you know it was God intervening. You don't have to write a chapter or a paragraph, just write a quick note, like "God delivered groceries." Once you have your list, you can start expounding on each little note and develop a paragraph or a chapter. Maybe you stink at writing. It doesn't matter. Just do it. It's like singing. It is written to make a joyful noise. If you write it and share it, it is worship in the purest sense. Do it in spite of your fear. It's true, and you need to share it and forget about your flesh, pride, or fear. People would rather see a sermon than read one any day. Like someone said, "You may be the only Bible someone ever reads."

As you write down these accounts of His intervention, share your heart. Share your fears, and share your feelings. Share the encouragement you see in what He did. Share the tangible ways this can help others. And if possible, relate it back to the Bible we all use. It will shock you how many ways you will see similarities in your life to those of old, such as Daniel or David.

CHAPTER 21

A King's Delight

ONE OF THE things that you rarely hear people talk about is the playfulness of our Father. He has a heart of playfulness because I can see it with what He does through dreams and secret gifts.

If you read, you will see that God gives people dreams and keeps the meaning a secret. This is truly a playful spirit of His. It's part of an interaction He has with us. How awesome it is that He is willing to take His time and play puzzles with us. This has become one of my favorite parts of my life. I love trying to figure out what the meaning is in a dream He gives me or someone close to me.

Please understand that I do not believe every dream is from God, but I can tell you that once you start paying attention, He will play the game more and more. It is quite fascinating to watch. There are so many wordplays that He will use. It is literally a lot of fun. My son Ben had a dream, and He was going to a "university where a lamb was the mascot." I giggled as he shared this with me. My son is new to interpreting dreams and couldn't see the meaning. I will let you figure it out for yourself. It's more fun that way.

These dreams sometimes are literal, like when my wife, Michelle, dreamed that there were bridges floating down the Cedar River here in Iowa. A couple months later, in the summer of 2008, we experienced a massive flood. And as part of this horrible flood, there were bridges that were dislodged and of course floated downstream.

I know you may have wondered in times past what a dream meant and couldn't figure it out. I have been there too. Sometimes you can share these dreams with others, and they will help you solve the puzzle.

Sometimes these dreams have people that you know directly involved in the dream. I would encourage you to pray first. But if you feel peace about it, share the dream with that person because it might be an answer to a question for that person. That is always such a blessing to a person who is seeking answers.

This part is hard. There are times when you ponder a dream for a long time and never get it figured out. Sometimes you just have to tell God, "I can't solve it" and move on. Later He may show you, and maybe He won't. It's okay.

Because dreams can be pictures of things months and even years later, I would encourage you to write down your dreams in a diary or log. The faintest print is better than the brightest memory my friend Loxley used to remind me all the time.

I have to say, I have not been the best at this practice, but I can change.

My mother passed away a few years ago. And while she was alive, she told me several times about how she dreamed and saw my family living in this house that has a tremendous number of windows. We bought a house shortly after that. And although it was a beautiful home, it never struck me as a house with an unusual number of windows.

A couple of years went by, and our realtor called and said he had a house he wanted us to look at that was not listed on the market yet. You see, my wife and I have had nineteen children and still have ten children at home. We have never really fit into a house very well because of the sheer number of people. Well, this house had enough bedrooms and bathrooms, and we had the ability, through God's provision, to buy it.

A month after we were moved in, I was climbing up on a chair to close a window. I had just talked to a business associate from Cedar Rapids, whom I had told we moved out to Anamosa. As we talked, we realized that she knew which house I lived in, and she remarked about how many windows the house had. It occurred to me, as I closed the window, God had shown my dear mother the house we would live in someday. I would say, she probably prayed many days for us to have a house we would fit in well. God showed here that He was going to fulfill that prayer.

CHAPTER 22

Footbaths, Spaghetti, and Coatings

I MENTIONED SECRET gifts earlier. I firmly believe God is the best giver of gifts. His gifts are plentiful and probably more than one could ever count. And even if it is hard, we know we should count our blessings, which include His tangible gifts.

As I was driving to work one day, it occurred to me that it was my mother's birthday coming up on February 12. I thought to myself, *What should I get her?* The thought popped into my head of a footbath, like the ones you see with bubbles and heated water. Later we gave my mom the gift.

"Oh, how could you know? This is exactly what I have been wanting," she said in her excited voice.

Have you ever been sitting there, thinking, "I am so tired. I just can't cook," and the next thing you know, there is a knock at the door? There in front of you is a friend, holding a pot of spaghetti.

The character of God is a mystery for all of us to seek out and study. His gift-giving ability is truly remarkable. What I have discovered is that many times, His gifts are last-minute gifts that only He can bring. Financially, it has always brought me peace to have figured out this part of the character. There were so many times when a gift card showed up in the mail for groceries when we didn't have money.

Sometimes it is such a small gift. You could easily miss the miracle if you didn't have your God antenna on to pick it up. It could be a quarter on the sidewalk you needed for a parking meter. It could be a cup of coffee your coworker got inspired to buy you when your paycheck was gone, but you wanted something warm on a cold construction site. It is possibly a fellow stopping by that noticed your tire was low and offered to change it for you because you are physically unable.

There are times when the gifts are quite large. One time I was working at a trade show for the trucking industry in Louisville, Kentucky, which I am attending again in three days.

We were there to promote a roof coating we make for refrigeration trailers called Invisaflects Reflective Roof Technology. The coating reduces fuel consumption and saves money for the trucking company. While at this trade show, we had what seemed to be pretty meager success at best. Many of the people we talked to were not the decision-makers or only had one trailer. There was one gentleman that one of my associates, Matt, talked to, who ended up being the director of innovation for one of the top 10 food distributors in the country. After several rounds of tests, this company has decided to use our product, which is incredible.

While doing testing on the coatings, I shared some of my own testimony with the director of innovation. It was after this that the seed started to grow in my mind about how our personal stories of God's intervention can be so powerful.

The interesting thing about the Hebraic culture is that there is an obsession with recording things. Much of the Bible is this way. There are records of the number of soldiers, gold, days, weeks, seasons, kings, war, etc. The main thing we can learn from all of this is to be good recordkeepers of God's works in our life. I don't think this is limited to writing, as we can see with YouTube and social networks, we can make living records of what He has done. Live it. Record it. Share it.

CHAPTER 23

Your Ark

YOUR FIRST THOUGHT might be by looking at the title for this chapter that I am going to encourage you to build your own version of Noah's ark. Ha… not so. On the other hand, I am going to encourage you to build your own version of the ark of the covenant. If you will recall, God told Israel to build a sort of trunk to keep the artifacts of all He did for them. This ark included Aaron's staff that budded, a jar that contained manna, and the tablets containing the main commandments God had given them.

I won't go into the significance of each item that was placed in the ark in this book. The point is that certain things are so huge that God does for us that we should keep some piece of memorabilia as a permanent reminder of this faithfulness in our life. I'm not saying you have to build a box. Maybe these are things you keep on a mantle. Maybe you keep them in your closet, on a shelf set aside just for this purpose.

It's interesting how many people will hold on to trophies and even build large display cases for their trophies, yet they will have no reminders of the past from what was really most important, the events and workings of God in our lives. I have goals, and I have won lots of trophies in my life. My wife watched me get rid of many boxes of trophies shortly after we got married. I love the song my dad loved so much called *The Old Rugged Cross*. One of the lyrics reads, "'Til my trophies at last I lay down, I will cling to the old rugged cross." The difference between the trophies and the ark is that one is about us, and the other is about Him and us together. Every perfect gift is coming down from heaven, above it is written.

So when you get healed of cancer, put that X-ray where the cancer used to be into your ark. I have a friend whose wife had a tumor on her brain. His wife had a lot of people praying for her because my friend and his wife have a ministry that has touched a lot of people. One day, his wife saw a flash, and the next appointment with the cancer doctor revealed the cancer was gone. But there was still an indentation on the brain where it had been. The doctor was not a believer in God. He said in very plain terms, "This is a miracle. There is no other way to put it."

When you grow up in poverty, in a one-bedroom house, wondering where you might get your next meal, and cashing in pop cans to survive, and then

God blesses you with a mansion, put a picture on the wall of that tiny house, and always remember the source of this great love and provision.

When you can't see, and all of a sudden, an evangelist prays for you, and you have sight, put that walking stick in a frame.

The wheelchair that used to cart you around is no longer needed. Take a picture of the chair, and look at it every day when you get out of bed and *walk* to breakfast.

The pain you felt for years because your loved one died is finally healed because God allows you a glimpse of them in heaven, having a blast. Paint a painting of the scene, and hang it on your living room wall.

Some perfect stranger walked up to you and told you how much God loves you on the day you were about to cash in your chips forever. Write a letter of remembrance to that wonderful soul that God used and put a copy in your drawer to review each day.

You roll your car three times in a freak accident and walk away without a scratch on you or your family. A gas can in the back lands straight and never even spills gas or causes a fire. Take a picture of the car and put it on your bulletin board at work.

Whatever you do, remember. Remember how much He has done for you. And if you can't remember, I would say you have been traveling through life unaware or possibly even deceived that everything has been a coincidence. This would be one of the biggest lies: to believe all those good things happened by accident. This is kind of like the lie and religion of evolution. The complexity of God's actions should never be relegated to chance because this is definitely a blasphemy of His Holy Spirit. Always give Him credit as it is definitely due to Him.

I have read that books for this genre are supposed to be a certain length. I have to say, I have never been good at conforming. I think each of you will write a book that may be unconventional or different. Please don't feel governed by rules. It is important that you begin this project and remember your content will touch many people's lives. And even if you never know that it has never changed anyone, that is okay.

I will conclude by saying this: The guy who preached to Billy Graham the night he accepted his Lord probably didn't know the significance of his sermon that night. How could he possibly know millions of lives were being affected that night.

There was a guy in Australia who witnessed to one person a day for many years, never knowing anyone ever received salvation. He gave them a Bible tract, and they moved on. Years went by, and two evangelists were talking and made the connection that tied back to this shopkeeper in Australia. Once again, millions of people were affected by this shopkeeper, who was oblivious to the ripple effect of his actions.

We are all planting seeds. God brings the sun and rain. We do our part, and He does His. In reality, of all the accomplishments a man or woman can make, nothing compares to the eternal consequences of our seed planting. Nothing at all matters more.

Be bold! Be brave! Share your story with anyone and everyone. It is powerful and life-changing! My friend Victor likes to say, "Facts tell, and stories sell." Tell your story, and help others get sold on the best thing that has ever happened to them.

I promise you more fulfillment in this quest than any other thing you will undertake. Yeshua said, "If you can't believe me, then at least believe the miracles." You are a miracle for someone.

Lastly, I recently heard an admonition from a famous atheist, saying that he would find it repulsive that a Christian would not tell him about God if that Christian believes in heaven and hell. Wow! That hit me upside the head, like a dirty two-by-four. In effect, that atheist will lead millions to the Lord, I believe. We have to line up what we really believe and get serious about it. Is hell real? Is heaven real? Is God real? If it is a yes, then we all have a duty to love others by doing our best job to show God to the world. It's not condemnation that we share. The world is already condemned in the words of Yeshua.

The problem is, so many don't know God is real. Make God a reality in someone else's life today!
    Let's go get this done!

MICHAEL W. TEMPLE is a serial entrepreneur, father to nineteen children, and husband to the best wife a man could ever find. Michael and Michelle live in Anamosa, Iowa, living a very busy life with many responsibilities.

He grew up in Waterloo, Iowa, attended Central High School, Wartburg College, University of Northern Iowa, and Kirkwood Community College.

He has a strong appreciation of music, art, and literature.

Michael founded Invisaflects in 2011, Energy Nerds in 2017.

Michael is passionate about seeing others find Yeshua and is hopeful that this book will lead many people to find salvation and share their Bible with others.

Michael has also written other works including the *Meandus of Yoreville* and "The Elijah Test."